White Lies & Other Truths

t.l. evans

BookLeaf Publishing

India | USA | UK

White Lies & Other Truths © 2022 t.l. evans

All rights reserved.

No part of this publication may be reproduced, stored in a retrieval system, or transmitted, in any form or by any means, electronic, mechanical, photocopying, recording or otherwise, without the prior written permission of the presenters.

t.l. evans asserts the moral right to be identified as author of this work.

Presentation by *BookLeaf Publishing*

Web: www.bookleafpub.com

E-mail: info@bookleafpub.com

ISBN: 9789357446808

First edition 2022

DEDICATION

First to the readers that live with chronic pain: you are warriors. The strength we have is unmatched, do not forget you are made of more than what hurts you.

Second to the readers who struggle with self-love, be gentle, for you cannot love others if you don't love yourself first.

And lastly, to the readers that are searching for a companion in this lonely world, I hope you find a friend in these pages.

ACKNOWLEDGEMENT

A thank you is in order to a number of people who helped me through this journey: the publishing team at BookLeaf Publishing for the opportunity to make my writing dream come true, to my beautiful family who have been my biggest supporters from day one, to my creative sister who designed the cover of this book and finally to my incredible partner, for believing in me especially on the days I doubt myself.

CONTENTS

PREFACE

My heart
Is in your hands
Be gentle with these pages
If you can relate to these poems
Half of me is sorry
The other half rejoices
Whether you feel my pain
Or celebrate my happiness
None of it matters
After all
Seven billion people only search for one thing
Relatability

CHAPTER 1
Bruises

The child's waiting room

She called me a veteran
But I've won no war
I'm fighting a battle with myself
And how can I win
When half of me sinks
And half of me swims

Chronic pain

Living in a body
That constantly betrays me
Is exhausting
How much longer
Can I keep begging for it to heal
When all it does is
Hurt

September sadness

That morning I questioned God
Why
Why do I live in a wreck of a body
I'm sorry for the sins I committed to deserve this
I feel hollow
Why don't I work?

Undiagnosed

The stare she gave me
Wasn't unfamiliar
Sympathy masking pity
I feel so fragile
Her lips are moving
But her words are empty
I'm sick of your condolences
Stop
Give me a diagnosis instead

Sick days

If only it was easy
Leaving the best part of me behind
The saddest part is
You were never a distraction
But you did distract me momentarily
From the life I couldn't stand
You made it bearable for a while
My mornings had purpose
There was a reason to wake up
Thank you
I promise the pain will fade one day
Hurting you was never my intention
But either was falling irrevocably in love with
you
I can't unsee myself as a malady
And you aren't the medicine

CHAPTER 2

Butterflies

Perfection

The way we were this afternoon
Is how we've always been in my head
Chest to chest
The room glowing golden around us
Eye contact that says more
Than words ever could
Your fingers tracing the outline of my face
Stolen kisses and soft smiles
Your arms feel like the safest place in the world

Hold me forever

I still get butterflies
Every time you walk into a room
But then you hold me
Our bodies pressed so tight
We're almost one
Our lips close but not touching
One hand on my spine
And the other in my hair
There is no safer place in this world
Than your arms

Love used to be four letters

Nothing is more precious
Than the seconds before we kiss
Your smile is my favourite thing
In the entire world
My heart still skips a beat
When you say you love me
I'm still half waiting for someone to shake me
awake
One morning soon
Saying I overslept
That this was all just a dream
That we were just in my imagination
When you aren't here some nights
I watch the stars through my window
Comforted by the thought
That although we aren't together
We're under the same sky

The truth

Mattering to someone never
Meant anything to me
Before I met
You

You make heartbreak seem less terrifying

Tonight was the first time
In my entire life
That I wasn't opposed to heartbreak
Because now I know
For a heart to break
It had to love
And be loved
First

CHAPTER 3
Breaking

Sunday night

This loneliness is swallowing me whole
And I'm tired of being eaten alive
By unrequited feelings
And wasted emotions

My biggest enemy is myself

I've always envied those comfortable in their
own skin
How do you make a home out of yourself
I long to ask
Do your flaws not bother you
Teach me how to silence the sharp thoughts in
my head
Jealousy is an understatement of what I feel
When I see that people are their own best friends

Stagnant

Loving someone
While hating yourself at the same time
Is exhausting
Seeing your best friend and worst enemy in the
mirror
Is confusing
How can I love him
And loathe me
All at once
How can I be
Breaking and healing
In the same moment

Loneliness

When he kissed me
I felt nothing
When she held my hand
I wanted to tear it away
The restaurant was too loud
Too many soundless voices merging
Creating a deafening suffocating cacophony
How can sitting next to my friends
Be so lonely
How can everyone around me
Speak the same language
Yet I don't understand

Cookie cutter

The older I get
I realise how similar people are
As if everyone was made of the same dough
Rolled thin
Onto the baking sheet of life
Cut from a perfect cookie cutter
Millions of gingerbread men
Fill this world
Each one no different from the next
I mourned because I was made from a different
dough
For so long I yearned
To be a gingerbread man
Only now I realise
There is nothing worse than being
The same as everyone else

CHAPTER 4

Blooming

You're my language

I'm at a loss for words
And the only way I can get them back
Is if you kiss me again

Our future

All I hope is that when we're old
Your heart still skips a beat
When I smile
You say I make you speechless
So I hope one day
You'll still be breathless with awe
Not age
I hope my hands are the only ones
You ever want to hold

The type of lover I want my sister to fall for

What kind of man
Are you
One day I hope my sister meets someone
With your understanding
And the soft tenderness in your eyes
I hope she feels as safe in another's arms
As I do in yours
If she doesn't get butterflies
When he smiles
He's the wrong man

You want to be his only comfort

One day you will realise
That you are in love with him
Not because of how he looks
Or touches or tastes
But because when he is upset
You would give the whole world to make him
smile again
And when he is angry at you
A hole opens in your chest
Only his forgiveness can fill
When his self-doubt swallows him
And his eyes won't meet yours
You feel ill that he doesn't see himself
As you see him

I wonder if you feel the same

I couldn't think of a worse punishment
Than not being able to stand by your side
For the rest of my life

How to make me fall in love with you

Put your hands on my mind
Before my waist
Wrestle with my thoughts
Before my tongue
Kiss the sad parts of me
Before my lips

www.ingramcontent.com/pod-product-compliance
Lightning Source LLC
La Vergne TN
LVHW010924200726
843509LV00013B/2066